Finding the Person in the Horoscope

Zipporah Pottenger Dobyns, Ph.D

Copyright 2012 by CRCS
All rights reserved.

No part of this book may be reproduced or transcribed in any form or by any means, electronic or mechanical, including photocopying or recording or by any information storage and retrieval system without written permission from the author and publisher, except in the case of brief quotations embodied in critical reviews and articles. Requests and inquiries may be mailed to: American Federation of Astrologers, Inc., 6535 S. Rural Road, Tempe, AZ 85283.

ISBN-10: 0-86690-631-2
ISBN-13: 978-0-86690-631-9

Cover Design: Jack Cipolla

Published by:
American Federation of Astrologers, Inc.
6535 S. Rural Road
Tempe, AZ 85283

www.astrologers.com

Printed in the United States of America

Contents

Chapter One, Choose Your World	1
Assumptions create reality	2
Materialistic vs. Humanistic Astrology	3
Chapter Two, Astrology's 12-letter Alphabet	7
Alphabet soup	8
An Example: Virgo Sun	8
Don't Forget the Houses	9
The Exaltation Fallacy	10
We Need All Twelve	12
Chapter Three, Elements and Qualities	13
Elements	14
Element Combinations	16
Qualities	18
Chapter Four, The Right Thing in the Wrong Place	21
Neptune in the Seventh	21
Saturn in the Seventh	22
Chapter Five, Astrological Dilemmas	25
The Cardinal Dilemma	26
In Defense of Saturn	27
Solving the Problem	28

The Fixed Dilemma	29
Self-mastery Through Sharing	29
Gate to the Universals	30
Sisterhood/Brotherhood	32
Freedom vs. Closeness	32
The Mutable Dilemma—World of the Mind	33
Search for Absolutes	33
Chapter Six, New Developments	37
Aspects	37
Asteroids	40
Ceres	41
Vesta	41
Juno and Pallas	42
Vertex Axis	43
Dwads and Decanates	44
Planetary Nodes	45
Fixed Stars	46
Midpoints and Arabic Parts	46
Sorting the Alphabet Soup	47
Is Once Enough?	50
Chapter Seven, The Alphabet in Action	51
Chapter Eight, Ethical Astrology	57
Appendix I, The Astrological Alphabet	59
House-Planet-Sign Combinations	59
Key Phrases for House-Planet-Sign Combinations	61
Aspects	65

Chapter One

Choose Your World

> "... we are witnessing the life and death struggle of two basic belief systems. One of these worldviews accepts life-consciousness as the creative power, and sees it evolving and testing its power through the manipulation of physical matterenergy."
>
> "The other world-view sees matter-energy as the final reality with life as an accident and consciousness as an epiphenomenon in a meaningless world."

Your world is your reflection of your understanding. Today we are witnessing the life and death struggle of two basic belief systems. One of these worldviews accepts life-consciousness as the creative power, and sees it evolving and testing its power through the manipulation of physical matter-energy.

The other worldview sees matter-energy as the final reality with life as an accident and consciousness as an epiphenomenon in a meaningless world. The first theory is accepted by most of the world's religions, whether they are sub-classified as theist, deist, pantheist, spiritualist, or something else. The second theory, which is labeled materialism, has been the conscious or unconscious assumption underlying most of modern science.

Assumptions Create Reality

Unfortunately, many scientists fail to realize that the facts, which are the coin of their realm, depend on their theory. That unproven theory or set of assumptions about the nature of reality determines which of the human experiences can be admitted as a fact and which experiences must be dismissed as chance, coincidence, illusion, fraud, etc. The same experiences are interpreted in totally different ways by individuals holding different beliefs about the nature of the world.

For example, a mystical experience is defined as merging with an impersonal absolute by the pantheist, as contacting a personal God by the theist, as a psychotic delusion by the materialist. Who is right? Who knows? Maybe they are all right. People may only be able to experience what their belief system permits them to experience! An atheist who denies the possibility of God as a reality can never experience God because a real contact with God would be defined as something else, perhaps an upset stomach. Remember the story of the man who made his first visit to a zoo and saw his first giraffe. After a long, incredulous look, he walked away muttering firmly, "There ain't no such animal."

Despite a century of scientific research with extrasensory perception which has produced odds of millions to one against the phenomena occurring by chance, many materialistic scientists still dismiss E.S.P. as "error some place."

The problem is further complicated by the fact that beliefs or assumptions are often unconscious rather than clearly conceptualized. Since attitudes, values, goals, choices, and consequent actions all depend on what the person believes to be true, real, morally right, possible, and desirable, this relegation of beliefs to the unconscious is asking for trouble. The potential for self-defeating actions is especially likely where conscious and unconscious beliefs and desires are in conflict. In such a contest, the unconscious almost always wins, and the person asks plaintively, "Why did that happen to me?" Or says, "I don't know why I did that. It is not like me."

Materialistic vs. Humanistic Astrology

Like the rest of the world, astrology today is split between these two basic worldviews. Materialistic astrologers believe that the material world is the power, and see all things, including people, as objects, as puppets manipulated by cosmic forces outside their control. Sidereal astrology is especially prone to this view of deterministic forces radiating from the visible stars. A number of other schools of astrologers such as the Uranians and cosmobiologists also focus primarily upon attempts to predict specific events.

The implicit or explicit belief behind such efforts is usually the materialistic assumption that the power of matter-energy determines what happens in the cosmos. The world is seen as a closed system with every future event already fore-ordained by the nature of the cosmos. Human beings are flies caught in this web of cosmic forces, with a character laid on them by the accident of having been born into a certain heredity, environment, culture, historical moment, and horoscope.

Humanistic astrologers, in contrast, tend to recognize the potential of life-consciousness as a creative force operating in an open system. In this worldview, the goal of life involves transcending the past in order to manifest latent potentials. Although the person operates within a world of law that puts definite limits on actions, the humanistic astrologer believes that there are some options or choices and that these choices can make a difference. In this worldview, character is destiny, and when we change our character (our habitual attitudes, beliefs, and actions) we change our destiny.

Under the materialistic worldview, character change comes when suffering forces us to change. The humanistic view sees people as partially self-determining. As we increase our insight (degree of self-awareness) and self-mastery, we increase our power to change attitudes and actions and thus to partially control our destiny. We cannot rule the world, but we can rule ourselves if we want to. Feeling that we *ought* to change will produce few results, but when we want to change, we can.

It is possible to be a materialist and still accept some potential for self-determination in mature humans. This worldview sees the person as an accidental result of an environment and heredity (which can include the cosmic environment as shown in the horoscope) but acknowledges the power of self-consciousness to become self-directing. It is easier to accept self-determination in company with a belief in reincarnation. The theory of repeated lives (here on earth and elsewhere) suggests that we have created our own character at all times, and that when we want to change it, we can.

Obviously, the belief system we accept has a major impact on the type of astrology we will practice. Those who place the power in the planets will look for good days and bad days, hoping to avoid action in the negative periods and to be able to do what they like in the favorable times. Their primary orientation will be outward, to see what the planets are likely to do to them in the future.

Those who place the power in the person will see the horoscope as a mirror helping them to see their own nature more clearly. Their primary orientation will be inward, evaluating the consequences of their own nature and determining how it might be altered to achieve a more effective and fulfilling life.

For them, astrology is a blueprint of the soul at a moment in time, but the essence of life is growth toward an infinite potential. The power of life can be seen in a clump of grass which pushes to one side a slab in a cement sidewalk as it reaches for the sun. The grass is not self-conscious. Its nature is simply to grow toward the sun. Humans are self-conscious and may choose to use this potential to facilitate their growth.

The sky has been the map, the clock, and the compass of humanity since before recorded history. It is a part of the order of the cosmos, and it is visible, so that we can see the pervasive order more clearly than is possible in the complexities of earth. But this does not mean that the sky (stars or planets) creates the order, anymore than a road map creates a set of roads. Consciousness may be the creative force in the cosmic order as it is the source of the map and the roads.

Accepting responsibility for our own life—character and destiny—is the price of freedom. Materialism says there is no freedom, no dignity, no responsibility. You are a victim in a hostile or indifferent world, but if you are clever, you may manipulate it into giving you what you want. The spiritual worldview says there is no way you can trick the world to get what you have not earned or to escape what you have earned. You can change your attitudes and actions, however, and earn a more satisfying life—and the self-knowledge available through the study of astrology can play a vital role in your growth.

If you are firmly wedded to the materialistic world-view, you might as well stop reading here. The balance of this book will approach astrology from a humanistic theoretical base. In this system, there are no malefics. We live in a meaningful cosmos and every part of it has a necessary and valuable place in the whole.

Chapter Two

Astrology's 12-letter Alphabet

> *"Astrology divides . . . human nature . . . into twelve parts which may be thought of as twelve ways of being in the world, or twelve sides of lite, or twelve motivational drives, etc. In metaphorical terms, astrology presents a twelve-letter alphabet."*

Astrology is only one of many conceptual systems that can be used to understand life. Each of them gives a portion of the picture just as infrared, ultraviolet, color, and black and white photographs will show different aspects of the same reality.

Human nature can be divided into three parts as Freud does with the ego, id, and super-ego; or as Transactional Analysis does with the parent, adult, and child. Astrology divides it into twelve parts that can be thought of as twelve ways of being in the world, or twelve sides of life, or twelve motivational drives, etc. In metaphorical terms, astrology presents a twelve-letter alphabet. Enormous complexity is possible because there are several forms of the basic alphabet. Planets, zodiacal signs, and horoscope houses all offer major forms of the alphabet, while decanates, dwads, nodes, and possibly fixed stars offer minor forms of the same alphabet. Letter "A" however, is still "a" whether it is upper or lower case.

Thus, whether the first letter of the astrological alphabet is represented by Mars or its nodes, by the first house of the chart, by the sign Aries, or the Aries dwad of a sign, it is still the drive toward individual self-expression. "I do my thing."

Since any planet can be in any sign in any house, a real chart involves complicated mixtures of the twelve parts of life. If the student has a clear understanding of the basic alphabet, the mixtures can be analyzed logically, and a range of possible consequences can be deduced.

An Example: Virgo Sun

My own Sun sign, Virgo, can be used to illustrate the principles. The Sun represents the ego drives of the individual—our need to pour out emotional energy and receive an emotional response back from the world. We want to do more than we have done before and to be recognized for it, whether we seek love, applause, respect, power, fame, or whatever. Virgo represents the urge toward efficient functioning, whether the focus is efficiency in the job or an efficient body (good health). The situation is analyzed, flaws are sought and corrected, and the end result should be solid competence.

A similar combination can be achieved in the horoscope by putting the Sun in the sixth house, Virgo in the fifth house, or Leo in the sixth house. In any case, what we have is an individual who seeks to meet ego needs through efficient functioning. Where the work satisfies the ego needs, where the individual is using creative power in the job and is achieving recognition or approval, the personal needs are met and all is well. The individual is a workaholic and lives for the work.

If the job is not fulfilling the ego needs—if it is boring, unappreciated or unchallenging—the individual may turn to body efficiency and become the a freak. This response involves the promotion of healthful living and gaining attention for personal success in achieving health. "Eat natural foods, don't smoke or drink, get enough exercise, breathe deeply, etc."

Unfortunately, there is a third option. For those unable to attain a fulfilling job or good health, it is possible to draw attention for one's poor health or inefficient functioning. The hypochondriac's plaintive: "Look how sick I am!" is not the most satisfying way to get the limelight and exert power over others, but perhaps it is better than nothing.

Don't Forget the Houses

The same principles can be used with any combination of the different forms of the astrological alphabet: planets in signs, planets in houses, signs in houses. This does not mean that planets and signs and houses are the same, but that they signify the same parts of life in their own way. They symbolize twelve basic motivational drives that can be seen as character (habitual attitudes and actions) and consequent destiny.

Traditional astrology has recognized that planets and signs represent both the character-personality and the events that stem from that character. Astrologers have tended to read houses as simply events. Work with psychologists has demonstrated that houses are also major keys to character. The houses may be read as basically the same as the signs that fall there with a natural zodiac; i.e., first house like Aries, second house like Taurus, third house like Gemini, etc.

The only combination giving the pure qualities of a single letter of the astrological alphabet occurs when a planet is in the sign it rules in the house of the natural zodiac associated with that sign. Thus, in order to get "pure Aries," we must have Mars in Aries in the first house.

General astrology tends to exaggerate the qualities of the signs since the focus is mainly on Sun signs. Placing the Sun in a sign is equivalent to combining Leo with the nature of the sign. Naturally there will be enlargement, intensification, emotionality, power, drive, etc. added to the qualities of the sign.

The blend of a planet with a sign or a planet with a house is similar to a conjunction between that planet and the natural ruler of the sign or house. Thus Mars in Capricorn, Saturn in Aries, Mars in the tenth house, Aries in the tenth house, Saturn in the first house, and Capricorn in the first house, are all similar to a Mars-Saturn conjunction.

The combinations are not identical because the planets are the power, like a verb in a sentence. But all of these combinations represent a blend of letters one and ten of the astrological alphabet, i.e, a combination of personal will and the limits of personal will whether these limits are imposed on us by the world or are voluntarily accepted through self-discipline. Any such combination may be positive or negative, depending on how the individual handles it.

The Exaltation Fallacy

Obviously, once this principle is recognized, the ancient exaltations seem questionable. It makes very little sense to consider Mars in Capricorn as the best possible position for this planet, Saturn in Aries as a difficult position, and a Mars-Saturn conjunction as terrifying—as is written in most astrology books.

The dignities were apparently assigned to the planets during the Arian age when the male warrior was the supreme value, and they reflect the ethical principles of that period. They seem out of place in a democratic age, whether we consider ourselves to be still in the Piscean age or verging on the Aquarian. The exaltation of the Sun in Aries was appropriate when Gilgamesh and Horner's epics were the role models for humanity.

Air signs, with their capacity for compromise, cooperation, talking things over, taking turns, etc., were considered weak and shameful. Mars, representing personal initiative, courage, self-willed action, when placed in Capricorn, could indicate the warrior who made his own will into law.

In the present age, where such action is disapproved, the individual is apt to run into a buzz saw if this overdrive is maintained. But at least equally often, Mars in Capricorn today signifies a person who is too self-blocking, sometimes to the point of illness. The aggressive drive to do one's own thing may be turned inward under the pressure of social and moral principles that emphasize love of one's neighbors.

In the Arian age, women were possessions along with the house and domestic animals. Jupiter as the key to trust and ultimate value was favored in Cancer, which symbolized the home and kin group as an oasis of security in a hostile world. And what does a warrior hero want in his females? His sex object (Venus) should be pliant, seductive, sensuous (in Pisces). But the wife who would bear his children and work in the fields or house should be strong-backed, placid, fertile, and patient (Moon in Taurus).

The Moon and Cancer were home and mother first, wife later, with Libra signifying open enemies and competitors. Saturn in Libra was desired since it offered the pleasant hope that the power of the law in some form would come down on the enemies. Ancient traditions show little understanding of the positive side of Saturn, dismissing it as the great malefic. The best that could be hoped from it was that the power would be directed against one's enemies and bring them to their knees. Wars are still with us, though becoming increasingly unpopular, but the ethics of the warrior hero were supposedly replaced nearly 2,000 years ago by the Christian principles of the Golden Rule. Why are we still stuck with the dignities?

A general rule of thumb can be suggested for the various combinations of planets with signs or houses. There is apt to be stress or tension of some sort whenever a cardinal or fixed planet is in a sign or house square or opposite its own sign or house. Normally, squares and fire-water combinations are the most difficult with the exception of letter ten (Saturn, Capricorn, tenth house), which can be a challenge even with planets, signs, and houses that are sextile its own. Planets in signs or houses quincunx their own natural sign or house can also be difficult to integrate. Combinations of mutables that would normally be square or opposite each other are less challenging, although they have their own dilemma.

We Need All Twelve

Remember that each of the twelve parts of life is a necessary part of the whole and is potentially valuable and satisfying. Everyone has some capacity for handling all twelve parts of life since we all have all of the planets, regardless of the distribution of power in signs and houses.

However, we can have problems if we are imbalanced with too much emphasis on a fragment of life and a lack of capacity to handle other parts of life. Or we can be in conflict between two or more parts of life, as is shown by squares, oppositions, etc. In such a case, it is necessary to integrate by making sure that we have an appropriate way to express each of these parts of life. It is also possible to attempt to satisfy one of these basic drives in the wrong place or time. Examples will be given of all of these potential problem areas.

Chapter Three

Elements and Qualities

"FIRE is the element that initiates action. EARTH follows fire and symbolizes the capacity to handle the physical world. AIR is next. After the life urge has poured out in some form of personal expression, air pulls back from this experience and looks at what has happened, thinks about it, talks about it. WATER completes the cycle and marks the stage of absorption and assimilation."

The initial problem of the astrologer is to find the person who is hiding behind the mass of little details in the horoscope. Popular astrology, with its emphasis on Sun signs, is apt to lose the unique person: "You're a Cancer. That takes care of you. Now I don't have to look at you anymore."

Genuine astrology, seeing each person as unique, has to try to organize the enormous complexity to avoid being lost in superficial fragments and contradictions. One of the helpful ways to synthesize the horoscope involves analysis of element and quality power, both individually and in combinations.

It is often possible to characterize a person as dominated by a single element or by a pair of elements or qualities. It is not possible for any element or quality to be totally missing, since all of the planets are present and carry their own quality, but there may be excessive emphasis on one or more elements or qualities with weakness in others which will indicate characteristic problems.

Elements

Fire is the element that initiates action. It is expressed emotion. Fire says: "I know what I want and I have the power to go get it." It is creative, confident, dramatic, exuberant, magnetic, and enthusiastic, with an irrepressible love of life. When fire is too strong the individual may be foolhardy, over-confident, and too self-centered and intent on meeting personal needs.

Yet it is often the generous element since its possessors have faith in themselves or in life and in their power to always get more.

Fire is insatiably restless, with a quest for novelty and a feeling of personal outreach. Where it is weak, there is often a lack of confidence and the courage for self-expression as an individual. The zest and humor and joy of living are diminished.

Earth follows fire and symbolizes the capacity to handle the physical world. It is practical, realistic, thorough, productive. The last two earth signs are the workers, representing all the Puritan virtues. Taurus is the capacity to enjoy the world of the physical senses. But all the earth planets, signs, and houses have the urge to produce something in tangible form.

Where earth is strong, the individual is likely to be successful in the physical world. Where it is too weak, there may be great talent but nothing productive is done with the ability.

Air is next. After the life urge has poured out in some form of personal expression with fire and met the physical world with earth, air pulls back from this experience and looks at what has happened, thinks about it, talks about it. Air symbolizes the conscious reasoning mind, the power to learn and to communicate. Air is the spectator.

Where there is too much air, the individual may spend most of the life observing and talking. Where there is too little there may be trouble in detaching oneself from situations and being truly objective, or trouble in dealing with peers.

Air is the only element able to really talk things over and compromise and take turns, to be a partner. Sometimes it is essential to say, "I've done my bit. Someone else can take over now."

Water completes the cycle and marks the stage of absorption and assimilation. Water represents the unconscious with its store of automatisms from the past—memories in the unconscious mind, habit patterns built into the functioning. It also represents the process of working with experience, keeping what is functional and letting go of the rest; but when there is too much water, it is almost impossible to let go.

The natural urge of water is to take in, just as fire's urge is to pour out. Water is the great caretaker, whether of people, things, institutions, or memories. As key to the unconscious, it is the psychic element since it is through the unconscious that we have access to the world beyond the physical senses and logic. This natural openness makes it the most vulnerable of the elements, like raw flesh with the skin off.

Water is also dependent, seeking a sheltering matrix while its attention is focused on the inner world. This can operate as a double-bind since there is simultaneously a need for the shelter and security of attachment but also a need to be alone in order to properly digest past experience. Like the cow chewing its cud, water brings back the past and works it over, seeking to assimilate what is of value so that it is no longer necessary to spend conscious effort on the action. It can be relegated to the unconscious, and the individual closes the chapter, ready for a new beginning with the fire that follows water in the endless cycle.

Too much water is probably the most difficult of the element imbalances. Such people are apt to be too sensitive, and if they remain dependent, they may continue to feel inadequate, anxious, and periodically depressed. Too little water marks the person lacking empathy and compassion, the capacity to feel with others. Favorable aspects between water planets especially mark the natural psychics, mystics, and healers. Where strength is shown by adequate earth, the individuals will shift from dependency to nurturance.

Remember that it is not sufficient to count occupied signs to assess element strength. Planets in fire houses add fire to the nature. Prominence of planets by angularity, numerous aspects, elevation, etc. adds to the power of their element. A water planet on the Ascendant or in the first house indicates extreme sensitivity, whether or not there are water signs present or planets in water houses.

Element Combinations

In addition to the analysis of the power of single elements, it is frequently possible to characterize a person by a preponderance of a combination of two elements. The qualities associated with pairs of elements can be deduced from the real materials for which they were named.

Fire-earth combinations can be imagined as a molten lava flow. This is the steamroller, the most creative and productive of the combinations with the initiative and creativity of fire and the practicality of earth with its urge to produce in tangible form. Fire-earth has an impact on the world and is still going when everyone else is dropping by the wayside.

Fire-air gives us hot air. These are the elements of self-expression. This is the super-salesperson and original rolling stone, the most fun of all combinations, with a keen sense of humor and incredible verbal facility. But if you have problems, don't bother telling them to the fire-air.

They don't want to be pulled down from their high, and are likely to leave if you get down. So they're the life of the party but not so much fun to live with. They are not sure they want to live with the same person for very long anyway.

Fire-water produces steam, and it can be scalding. This is the emotional yo-yo, with heavy mood swings, from euphoric when the energy is expressing out in successful action, to depressed and miserable when they are thrown back into the water. There is often a stop-go, staccato quality about the nature. The water holds emotions in until the pressure builds up to the point where there is an explosion.

Fire and water are the emotional elements, and the feelings are super-intense when they are combined and emphasized in the chart. There is also apt to be an inner battle between the fire urge to be a free soul and the water urge to be attached.

Leo is an exception among the fire signs since it needs emotional responses from others, while Pisces is sometimes an exception among the water signs since it can attach itself to God or a "cause" and avoid dependence on human beings. But individuals with strong fire and water are always warm, caring people.

Earth-air, the rational elements, give us the opposite of fire-water—the person with minimal feeling. Everything is objective and logical and realistic. The combination produces dust, and the people can be pedantic and dry as dust. But it is a highly valuable mixture for a CPA, tax attorney, or any precise work.

Earth and water can make mud or wet cement. Where they are emphasized we have the mothers and fathers and saviors of the world. With the urge of earth to carry the load and the need for attachment and closeness of water, the combination is almost always nurturant.

Here you find the Atlas syndrome, carrying the world on the shoulders. If you need help, look for an earth-water person. They may complain, but they will take your burden on their backs. But it is a heavy combination. They take themselves and life too seriously in their urge toward preservation.

Air and water are mist, fog, vapor. Air-water people may live in their heads and never do anything else. They make fantastic psychotherapists with the ability to tune in to the unconscious and then to bring it into consciousness and communicate it. But unless there is some strength from fire or earth, they are floaters, drifters, dreamers.

Qualities

The qualities—cardinal, fixed, and mutable—give us the grand crosses of astrology because signs or houses of the same quality fall opposite or square each other.

A quick way to portray the essential nature of the qualities is to imagine two cars reaching an intersection simultaneously, on a collision course with each other. The cardinal cars arrive, crash, one flips on its back and the other charges off at a new angle. If Aries or Mars or the first house is involved, the crash may follow a high-speed approach. If Cancer, the Moon, or the fourth house and Saturn, Capricorn, or the tenth house are solely involved without the air-fire cardinals, the speed is low but the momentum irresistable.

Fire and air seek change, while water and earth cling to the status quo and change often comes despite their desires. The change may be a result of past actions with the consequences working out in the present, or it may be due to unconscious desires. Remember, when there is a conflict between conscious and unconscious, the latter usually wins. In any case, the cardinal planets, signs, and houses are likely to bring events: overt changes in the life.

The fixed cars approach the intersection at a snail's pace for water-earth and with more speed, but again mainly determined momentum, for fire-air. They get their noses together and hold, in a state of impasse with neither giving an inch.

The more emphasis on fixed planets, signs, and houses, the more likely the person is to stay in a stalemate situation and just live with it. If fire and air are involved without the restraining hand of earth–water, change will come but on the terms of the individual. Fixed signs represent enduring self-will.

The mutable cars never get close enough to each other to touch. One car veers in one direction and the other goes around it and they circle and try again in a kind of dance. Mutables live in the head, with a flexibility and versatility that promotes constant change; but at the same time a lot of their experience is vicarious through reading, thinking, and observing other people. There may be an over-sensitive nervous system and a tendency for allergies.

When two qualities are strong there can also be characteristic manifestations. A mixture of cardinal and fixed tends to set life up as a perpetual power struggle. Persons having this emphasis may need to concentrate on learning to relax and observe and flow with life, to be more flexible. A mixture of cardinal and mutable is apt to mean too much restlessness and need for change. People with this tendency often have to work to achieve stability in the life. There are often nervous tensions and a general lack of rootedness. The fixed and mutable mixture is less easy to characterize. Individuals with this combination may be basically stable but possess restless minds, or they may experience change vicariously through relationships.

Since most charts will have a mixture of qualities such as cardinal planets in fixed signs in mutable houses, it is often impossible to be sure whether a pattern will produce overt events or an emotional impasse or a head trip. Since the angles of the chart operate rather like the cardinal planets, aspects to natal or progressed angles are likely to indicate overt events.

The Ascendant is similar to another Mars in the chart and shows personal action, while the Midheaven acts as another Saturn, lifting us up to power or putting us down if we have over-reached and bitten off more than we can chew. The third angle-axis, the Vertex and Anti-Vertex, will be discussed later. Since it can fall in any type of house (cardinal, fixed, or mutable) it is not inevitably a key to overt events, but more often than not, strong aspects to either natal or progressed Vertex will show events involving other people in the life.

Naturally, elements must also be taken into account. Water may focus inward and show few external signs of the inner ferment. Air will talk about the situation but may not do anything more. Earth will want a tangible result, and fire simply wants to pour out its own urges, whether they express primarily in action (Aries), emotion (Leo), or thought (Sagittarius). The goal of humanistic astrology is to find the person in the midst of all the details. Synthesis is an art that takes years of practice, but a clear understanding of the principles of astrology gives a solid foundation for the accomplishment.

Chapter Four

The Right Thing in the Wrong Place

"One of the sources of problems in life involves looking for satisfactions in the wrong places."

One of the sources of problems in life involves looking for satisfaction in the wrong places. Placement of planets in signs and especially in houses that are square, opposite, or quincunx their own signs or houses may show this misplaced aim.

Neptune in the Seventh

For example, Neptune symbolizes the urge for mystical oneness with life or God. Letter twelve in all forms (planet, sign, house) is searching for an emotional absolute—for infinite love and beauty. When Neptune is placed in the seventh house, or Pisces is in the seventh, or Neptune is in Libra, or the ruler of the seventh house in the twelfth house, and so on, we are looking for a partner to give us this experience of mystical fusion and total emotional absorption and ecstacy.

But a true partnership is a peer relationship permitting open communication and compromise between equal human beings. The consequences of searching for God in a human partner may be varied, but almost always somewhat frustrating.

Some people project their dreams of infinite love and beauty onto potential partners and fail to see the real individuals, only to wake up later disillusioned and disappointed when the partners fail to live up to their ideals. Another person may search for the perfect partner and never marry since no human ever meets standards. Where the personal relationship is highly important, the subject may marry repeatedly, each time hoping for the perfect "made in heaven" match.

Still another variation is to search for someone to whom we can play God rather than someone to be God for us. This type of person chooses a victim, someone who needs to be saved, such as an alcoholic, drug addict, psychotic, or chronic invalid. But the relationship is apt to end in disaster since marriage based on feeling sorry for someone is an ego put-down for the victim. Even when the motivation is unconscious (as it usually is) the victim may eventually respond by seeking to get even, and put down the other. This may be done by being unfaithful, by leaving, by attacking the other verbally, etc. Or the victim may simply become a super-victim. "You want someone to carry? I'll let you."

For people with the above or other variations on combinations of letters seven and twelve of the astrological alphabet, the best solution is to become a therapist and save people professionally. Any type of helping profession will do.

Saturn in the Seventh

Another illustration of the same principle is a combination of letters seven and ten. This can be present with Saturn in the seventh house, Saturn in Libra, Capricorn in the seventh house, Venus in Capricorn or in the tenth house or conjunct Saturn, etc.

Here, we are combining the urge toward an ongoing peer relationship (in contrast to the more casual and intermittant associations of letters three and eleven) with the power of letter ten. The combination may invite marriage to a father figure or the choice of a weak person to whom we will be father. There may be, on the other hand, fear of being dominated, rejected, criticized, or judged with consequent delay of partnership. There are often power struggles with loved ones when the "child" in the relationship gains sufficient confidence to challenge the "parent."

It is possible to maintain a balanced peer relationship if both partners take turns being parent and child. The same compromise can be reached with Moon or Cancer in the seventh house, or with Venus in Cancer, the ruler of the seventh house in the fourth house, or other combinations of letters four and seven. If the two persons become inter-dependent, there can be a warm and mutually supportive relationship, each giving to the other in areas of personal strength and receiving where the partner is strong.

Chapter Five

Astrological Dilemmas

"The essence of the cardinal dilemma can be described as the conflict between Aries Freedom (pure self-will), Cancer Closeness (baby-mother relationship), Libra Partnership (peer relationship), and Capricorn Control (Wielding power)."

The preceding discussion is actually a variation on what I have called the dilemmas. The conceptual view of life given to us in astrology divides human nature and life into twelve parts, as has been already noted. Some of these parts of life are naturally harmonious or complementary, and some clash by their nature.

The strongest inherent conflicts are between the signs that are square or quincunx each other. Opposing signs are natural partners, but there is still a tendency toward a separative action or swinging like a pendulum between them even though they represent two ends of a continuum, or a polar principle.

I call the three grand crosses of astrology the dilemmas: the cardinal, fixed, and mutable dilemmas. The word is chosen to point up the concept that these different parts of life do conflict with each other. We cannot do any two of them to the fullest extent at the same time and place. And yet they are each valuable and necessary for a whole life.

So the dilemma involves finding an appropriate time and place and way of satisfying all twelve of the basic drives of life. Once this is done there is no problem; the person is versatile and able to handle all of life effectively.

It is usually easier to integrate the conflicts between different parts of life than to develop the capacity to handle a part of life where this capacity is almost missing. Squares are therefore probably preferable to a seriously unbalanced chart.

The Cardinal Dilemma

The cardinal dilemma can be symbolized by stress aspects such as the square, opposition, quincunx, semisquare, sesquisquare, and conjunction. These aspects can occur between cardinal planets, or cardinal signs, or cardinal (angular) houses. As already noted, placing a cardinal planet in the sign or house of another cardinal planet (such as Mars in Capricorn) can be one form of the cardinal dilemma. This same principle holds for the fixed and mutable planets.

Any of these combinations can be successfully integrated by making an appropriate place in the life for the basic drives. This integration may involve expressing the nature of the factors at different times or places, or one may compromise and not express either factor to its fullest extent.

The essence of the cardinal dilemma can be described as the conflict between Aries freedom (pure self-will carried into immediate action with no concern for anyone else), Cancer closeness (a baby-mother relationship), Libra partnership (a peer relationship where each compromises in order to have harmony in joint action), and Capricorn control (wielding power whether control is sought for a sense of security or out of a feeling of responsibility). To express any one of these to the fullest extent, one must temporarily give up the others. Dependency loses the most.

Dependent persons lack freedom, equality, and control unless they are able to use their weakness as a means of control. Self-will, the freedom to do what we please, permits some feeling of control over the personal life but can only be approached when we are alone. Associations mean strings, no matter how lightly tied. True control includes self-control so impulse is curbed by self-discipline.

In Defense of Saturn

In view of the negative descriptions of Saturn in many astrology books, a fuller statement on letter ten seems needed. Saturn, Capricorn, and the tenth house all symbolize the structure of the world, which is largely outside of personal control.

This structure includes time, law on all levels from natural laws like gravity to the bureaucratic systems of society, the consequences of the past that cannot be changed, authority figures, and so on. Occult tradition calls Saturn the "Ring pass not" and it symbolizes the limits inherent in the nature of the cosmos. Our choice is whether to fight the limits with some form of overdrive that in effect seeks to make our own will into law or to voluntarily live within the limits—to be self-limiting. The last can also be overdone by excessive self-blocking and may be a source of illness.

On the physical level, Saturn is symbolic of the crystallized structures within the body such as the bones and teeth. At the mental level, it represents the self-discipline of the Puritan virtues such as duty, responsibility, thoroughness, practicality, organization, completion, and thrift. In society, it corresponds to executive power, whether dealing with other authority figures or wielding power oneself.

But note that in a democracy, the executive carries out the law; he or she does not make it. The legislature (Aquarius) makes the law: a body of peers meeting in cooperation. Freedom is possible only to the extent that we stay voluntarily within the limits of the laws of both nature and society. The law is bigger than we are, and in a contest the power symbolized by Saturn is going to win.

Letter ten in all forms represents what we can do, what we cannot do, and what we have to do. So long as we are doing our share voluntarily and realistically, there is no problem with Saturn. The law of cause and effect can only bring us what we have earned. A problem with Saturn is an indication that the individual is trying to get something he or she has not earned or is trying to get out of soemthing that has been earned.

Solving the Problem

The cardinal dilemma, whether shown in the chart by planets, signs, or houses, is resolved when the individual makes a place in life for free self-expression and initiative, for dependency-nurturance relationships, for ongoing cooperative peer relationships, and for a responsible role in society. If it is not resolved, the individual is likely to go in and out of relationships, homes, jobs, power struggles with authority figures, and sometimes illness.

Illness may be way to get out of doing what we do not want to do, or (where dependency needs have been severely repressed) it may be the only way we can let ourselves be taken care of. The most common solution to the cardinal dilemma is to play the mother-father role. This role permits the individual to be in control but also to have closeness, and he or she can take the freedom and permit equality when desired.

The only cardinal urge that must be denied is dependency. The dependency needs are still present, however, and must be dealt with. An inability to cope with certain areas (mechanical things, mathematics, maps, etc.) may be disguised dependency needs. Let the world help you. This is an age of specialization. But don't say that you can't do them. Say that you prefer to exchange services.

The Fixed Dilemma

The fixed dilemma is less likely to disrupt your life, and individuals may struggle with it in a state of stalemate for years. Two fixed signs, houses or planets at right angles are rather like the irresistible force and the immovable object. Periodically, when the power builds to sufficient intensity, there is an expolsion, but when the dust clears, the same old impasse may be still there with a few edges worn down.

The fixed letters of the astrological alphabet can be called the "self" ones. Taurus indicates self-indulgence; Leo marks the urge for self-expansion; Scorpio holds the potential for self-knowledge and self-mastery; Aquarius suggests self-proportion.

With Taurus we develop the capacity to enjoy the physical world, including the ability to create beauty and pleasure and comfort for ourselves and others. This is the most placid and contented sign in the zodiac—Ferdinand sitting in the field, smelling the flowers.

Leo, as already noted, shows our ego need to enlarge our world, feel our power, and have an emotional response from others. The Sun, Leo, and the fifth house show where we need to feel proud of ourselves. Sitting in a field is not enough; charge! Leo needs to make an impact on the world and to receive attention for it. But normally one lives with the dilemma and tries to meet the need for a sense of pride without sacrificing too much comfort. Or, if the creative power of Sun-Leo-fifth house has been expressed as procreation and we have produced a child, a major part of the Taurean comfort and material resources will have to be directed toward the child instead of the self. Similarly, if we choose to invest, speculate, or gamble, some of the current resources must be given up in hopes of the later and larger return.

Self-mastery Through Sharing

With Scorpio-Pluto-eighth house we are dealing with other people's resources, pleasures, and passions as Taurus marks our own, and we have to give up some of our own to have shared pleasure. The potential of letter eight is to learn self-knowledge through the mirror of another person and to learn self-mastery out of respect for the rights of the other.

The Taurus-Scorpio opposition is a continuation of the Aries-Libra polarity, where we learn to balance our own needs and pleasures against the needs and desires of the mate. We meet in open confrontation in Aries-Libra. In Taurus-Scorpio, the scene is shifted to the physical world—resources, pleasures, appetites, sensuality, etc., which are shared.

Taurus-Scorpio conflict aspects in any form may be experienced as tension over whether to earn one's own income and keep full control over it, or to be dependent on a mate. The tension may involve decisions on how to handle joint resources or pleasures. Who earns it? Who spends it? For what? What do we both enjoy?

At times the conflict may be totally inward in the struggle between appetite indulgence and appetite mastery. "I have the right to enjoy the physical world, but I ought to be master of my appetites." Such people may alternate between dieting and over-eating, smoking and trying to stop smoking, drinking and trying to limit drinking, sex and celibacy, spending and saving, and so on.

Gate to the Universals

Pluto, Scorpio, and the eighth house mark one of the great challenges of life. We need to learn to respect the rights of others in a close relationship before we are ready to deal with humanity as a whole (which we face in the last four signs).

Scorpio is the gate to the universals, where we meet the shadow (in Jungian terms) or the "dweller on the threshold" in occult terms, in the form of our own undigested and often partially buried garbage. Scorpio rules the end of the digestive process where we must make the final discrimination on what to keep and what to discard in our accumulated experiences of learning to deal with peer relationships through Virgo, Libra, and Scorpio.

With Scorpio, Pluto, and the eighth house, we must learn when to stop, how to let go, what belongs to us and what to others, how to love with an open hand, to control ourselves rather than others but not to over-control even ourselves. Scorpio can swing from excess to asceticism and back again in the battle. If the lesson is not learned, we may see the consequences in constipation at the body level or in events which take people or things from us.

This loss can occur through death, which forces us to learn to let go or to stand alone if excessive dependency is the problem. Scorpio is in a double-bind in its own nature, since it is a water sign and thus naturally driven by the need for fusion with another to satisfy strong dependency needs. "The world should care for me so that I can concentrate on my inner self-exploration." But at the same time, the need for mastery is urgent. Simultaneous dependency (which implies helplessness) and mastery are difficult to integrate.

Struggles between the various forms of letters five and eight are apt to be the most intense. There is a power drive in all fixed letters, whether planets, signs, or houses, but at each stage of the movement from Taurus to Aquarius, the power is limited a bit more. Taurus marks our own possessions; we have earned them and have the right to manipulate them for our own satisfaction.

In one sense Leo represents increased power because it symbolizes the king who has power over people. Leo, however, is self-limiting to the extent that there is a strong desire to have love and admiration from others, and this can hardly be won with disregard for their feelings.

Scorpio continues to work on learning to limit the power voluntarily. The practice takes place with a peer relationship, whether in marriage, with a business partner, in a therapeutic interaction such as counseling, or in other forms of joint action that involve physical possessions or sensuality.

Sisterhood/Brotherhood

The last fixed letter (Uranus, Aquarius, eleventh house) takes the final step of relinquishing all power over others, retaining only power over knowledge. Aquarius respects the right of all people to be free so long as they give the same right to others. Properly handled, Aquarius marks the stage of purely voluntary cooperation with everyone, with no coercion. But this is only possible if all concerned have accepted the self-discipline of Capricorn. Scorpio gives us the opportunity to learn self-mastery in a peer relationship, but if it is not learned there voluntarily, Capricorn puts the lid on through outside force. This is one of the sextiles that can be a difficult combination, or a dangerous one—mixtures of letters eight and ten.

As examples, President Richard Nixon had Pluto in the tenth house, while heiress (and kidnaping victim) Patricia Hearst has Saturn in Scorpio. Any such combination is a warning to be careful of the use of power so that we do not confuse personal will with law. The different forms of letter ten are always a warning to stay within the law or face the consequences.

Freedom vs. Closeness

The Leo-Aquarius polarity shows the pull between the king and the commoner. It shows the need for close, personal, intense love relationships versus the desire to hang loose with no strings and remain friends at a distance. It may mark the need to feel proud of oneself in conflict with the conviction that all humans should be equals, or the tension between an emotional life and an intellectual one.

The Scorpio-Aquarius contest can also indicate tension between a desire for a close, emotional relationship and a desire to hang loose. This basic freedom-closeness conflict is one of the most common of the human dilemmas and can be seen in many ways: Aries square Cancer,

Aquarius quincunx Cancer, Sagittarius quincunx Cancer, Aquarius square Scorpio, Aquarius opposition Leo, Aries opposition Libra, Aries quincunx Scorpio. Naturally, although only signs are mentioned here, the conflict may occur in the chart with planets or house position as well. It is cumbersome to list all three forms of the astrological alphabet each time, so signs are sometimes mentioned alone as a convenience.

The Mutable Dilemma—World of the Mind

The mutable dilemma operates in the world of the mind. The first two mutable letters represent the conscious, reasoning mind of Mercury. Gemini is the young curiousity that wants to know everything for the sake of knowing. Virgo is driven to use the knowledge for some productive result, so must narrow the range and focus on a small area. This is a minor conflict, and normally indicates someone who is over-extended-trying to know something about everything while still doing something useful with the knowledge in an area of specialization.

Search for Absolutes

The last two mutable letters are both ruled by Jupiter and they are looking beyond the here-and-now for some kind of absolute. Letter nine (including Jupiter, Sagittarius, and the ninth house) is searching for truth with a capital "T."

Sagittarius may search in books, schools, religion, philosophy, or science, or wander to the ends of the earth in the quest. The belief system accepted is vitally important, as was pointed out in the initial section of this book. Based on the individual's faith in what is true, real, morally right, possible, and desirable, the value hierarchy is set up, goals formulated, and choices made. Often the belief system is partially unconscious. We may look for our ultimate trust and value in a person, in money, in fame, in power, or in many other parts of life. Wherever Jupiter, Sagittarius, or the ninth house rulers fall, we are looking for God in some form.

The absolute of the ninth letter of the astrological alphabet can still be expressed in language if we choose to, while letter twelve in all forms is looking for an emotional absolute, for infinite love and beauty. If the individual is actively doing something to make the world more loving and beautiful, all is well. Letter twelve symbolizes the healers, helpers, artists, saviors, and mystics.

But if the person with a strong Neptune, Pisces, or twelfth house is not doing something to find the beautiful vision, he or she is apt to be the victim looking for the savior. Any variety of cop-out is possible, including drugs, alcohol, illness, or psychosis, as the person seeks the dream in an "easy" way, or tries to get someone else to provide it without personal effort. Pisces needs the patient, practical effort of Virgo to implement its vision, but Virgo equally needs the vision of Pisces to lift its eyes from the squirrel cage of daily duties and minute details.

Conflicts between letters nine and twelve may indicate contests between head goals and heart goals, or between the fire urge toward individual initiative and action versus the water urge toward dependency. This can be another freedom-involvement struggle.

A generalized mutable dilemma usually indicates a person who is immensely versatile with a multiplicity of interests and difficulty in deciding between them. The result is often a jack of all trades who lacks the persistence to really accomplish much.

With a mutable dilemma, it is vital to analyze what the person believes, values, trusts, and wants out of life, so that a focus and follow-through may be established. Sometimes the goals are quixotic and it is necessary to become more realistic about what is possible. In other cases, personal beliefs, values, and desires may be in conflict with the traditions of the society or with the values of close associates.

With an unresolved mutable dilemma, the person may get physically lost. Without clear values and goals, there is an inadequate sense of direction. In extreme cases, there may be psychotic breakdowns with a confusion between personal beliefs and the reality of the world. If there is adequate earth in the chart, the drive to produce something in tangible form will be present and the individual is likely to be frantically over-extended but still accomplishing something solid with the life.

Chapter Six

New Developments

"Astrology is probably the most complex and sophisticated method of describing life that has ever been discovered or developed by human beings. The whole pattern never repeats, and yet this infinite variability is achieved with the different forms of the twelve-letter alphabet...."

Aspects

Aspects are the angular distances between the planets. They have been a basic part of astrology for millennia, but much new information has been discovered in recent years. Classical astrology accepted all multiples of thirty degrees as valid aspects, denoting some type of interrelationship between the parts of life involved. The strongest aspects were said to be 0, 90, 120, and 180 degrees. Of these, only the 120 was considered entirely favorable, and the 90 was viewed as the most difficult.

Aspects are derived by dividing a circle by whole numbers: for example, dividing the 360 degree circle by two gives the opposition of 180 degrees, dividing it by four gives the square of 90 degrees, and so on.

In time, division of the circle by eight gave the semisquare (45 degrees) and its variant, the sequisquare (135 degrees, or three-eighths of the circle). The great astrologer-astronomer Johannes Kepler discovered that one-fifth of the circle gave a valid aspect: the quintile of 72 degrees. The biquintile (144 degrees), along with other variations including one-tenth and one-twentieth of a circle, stem from Kepler's work.

The most thorough research yet undertaken on aspects has been that of radio engineer John Nelson. Since the early 1950s, Nelson has worked almost full-time improving the methods of forecasting ionospheric disturbances that might disrupt short-wave radio transmission in the North Atlantic. In his painstaking work Nelson confirmed the classical aspects and discovered many other angles that he calls "harmonics" and that he finds add power to a configuration.

Nelson uses every multiple of 7½, 11¼, and 18 degrees, thus confirming the work of earlier researchers and helping to explain the added power of the 0, 90, and 180 degree angles, since all three series include these three aspects. Nelson found that the multiples of 30 degrees (including zero) are the most powerful, but that the added angles must be taken into account for accuracy. He maintained a five-year record of forecasting that did not fall below 92 percent accuracy. His forecasts were made at six-hour intervals on a six-point rating scale and published months ahead of the time for which he was predicting.

To attain such phenomenal accuracy, Nelson used only the angles between planets (including the Earth rather than the Moon). He worked heliocentrically, measuring the aspects as they would be seen from the position of the sun.

In addition to the angles listed above, Nelson confirmed the validity of midpoints or halfsums: i.e., the center point between any two factors in the chart. Nelson found that if a planet is on a midpoint, the power of the interaction is increased. He also found added power if a planet is on its own Node (where its orbit intersects the plane of the Earth's orbit) or on its own perihelion or aphelion (where it is closest to or farthest from the sun in its own orbit). Considerable work has also been done in Germany to support the midpoints and multiples of 7½ degrees.

Nelson's work has substantiated the ancient traditions of the harmony of the trine and the stressful nature of the square. In a personal conversation, he described two occasions when a solar storm (previously signaled by a combination of conjunction, square, and opposition) was in progress. At the height of the storm, a trine became exact between two planets not involved in the original storm configuration, and the sun storm died down "as if a hand had been laid on it," to quote Nelson's words.

He also commented that he never saw the really spectacular solar flares unless there were at least two exact multiples of 18 degrees between the planets. Planetary aspects thus provide a key to both solar activity and to ionospheric disturbances, but there is no exact correspondence between the sun and the Earth.

We are just beginning to test these additional harmonics in the charts of human beings, and the initial results seem to support the pioneering work of Nelson. Since people are far more complicated than the sun or the ionosphere, it is unlikely that we can hope to reach Nelson's level of accuracy. Nevertheless, these new aspects and midpoints are well worth investigating.

In another sense, adding the harmonics puts even more pressure on us to find answers to the question of permissible orb. There is enormous controversy over the issue of aspect orb. How far can the angle deviate from the exact degree and still be considered?

If we allow an orb of 10 degrees to a square, we have overlapped two harmonics: 82½ and 97½. If we allow a 12-degree orb for the square, we take in two more harmonics: 78¾ and 101¼. If we allow 15 degrees for a conjunction, as is taught in some astrological schools, we have covered the harmonics of 7½, 11¼, and 15 degrees. Extensive research is needed before we can settle this issue.

My own general guideline involves an examination of the chart to see whether a wide aspect indicates a character tendency that is shown in other ways in the chart. If there are other factors that point in the same direction, I accept the wide orb aspect as a further confirmation of this tendency. If the chart fails to show the personality inclination in other ways, I discount the wide orbs. It is of course possible that the powerful aspects such as the square do have a wide but diminishing area of overlap with increased strength in the area of the harmonics. Certainly we must limit the harmonics to a narrow orb—probably one degree at the most.

There may also be aspects at one-seventh of the circle (51.4+ degrees, the septile), at one-ninth of the circle (40 degrees, the novile), and at one-eleventh of the circle (32.72+ degrees, the undecile). Much additional work is needed to clarify and validate the principles, but the importance of aspects has been amply demonstrated by Nelson's accurate forecasts.

Asteroids

Ancient astrology knew of five planets plus the Sun and Moon, and the 12 signs and houses were divided between them, each planet ruling two signs and houses while the Sun and Moon had one each. As additional planets were discovered after the invention of the telescope, they were observed until their nature became clear and they could be linked to a sign and house. The latest to be seen, Pluto, is still involved in controversy over rulership, although most astrologers assign Pluto to Scorpio as is done in this book. So far, each time a new planet has been discovered, it has been given an appropriate name taken from a mythological god whose character fit the nature of the planet. The materialistic worldview cannot explain such an incredible "coincidence."

In the early years of the ninteenth century, four asteroids were discovered in orbit between Mars and Jupiter in an area that ought to contain a planet, according to Bode's Law. All four were named for mythological goddesses, but an ephemeris giving their zodiacal positions was only made available to astrologers in 1973. They have been observed by many astrologers since that date, and have been found to correspond closely to the goddesses for whom they were named.

The descriptions offered here are based on personal work, especially from noting the periods in subjects' lives when an asteroid was prominent and checking to see what type of event occurred at such times. At the time of this writing, these four asteroids have been personally observed in several hundred charts, and the qualities associated with them seem clear and established in my own experience. But until vast majority of astrologers have worked with them, there will undoubtedly continue to be uncertainty and differences of opinion.

Ceres

Ceres seems to be an earth-mother. It combines the qualities of Virgo and Cancer, with a devotion to personal service, including a strongly nurturing nature. It is usually prominent when individuals have children or are concerned with nurturing others. It can be thought of as the personal side of Virgo.

Vesta

The most dramatic cases in my work with the asteroids have involved Vesta, which seems to represent the impersonal side of Virgo. If an individual with a prominent Vesta is voluntarily dedicating his or her life to some sort of service, there is often great success, sometimes even in fields for which the person has little training or experience. The keynote is personal devotion to the work.

When people do not make such a commitment to their work, they are often unhappy in it. They may have serious problems with work or be forced to work against their will. Illness may result from work tensions, as a subconscious maneuver to escape the work. There may also be difficulties in personal relationships with a prominent Vesta. In some cases the whole life is given to service to the exclusion of the personal side of life.

When Vesta is emphasized in the current life, there are often separations from associates, whether through voluntary action in pulling back or through having people taken away by circumstances beyond personal control. President Nixon is an example of a powerful Vesta, especially during 1973-1974. The Watergate turmoil included all of the negative potentials of Vesta: stress connected to work, separations from many work associates, and health problems. But it is important to remember that Vesta's positive side is a responsible commitment to work and often outstanding success.

Juno and Pallas

Juno and Pallas seem connected to Libra, with Juno representing the personal side of Libra, especially associated with marriage, while Pallas is more impersonal. Pallas is often prominent in political charts or in people involved in politics. Teaching and counseling are also common.

However, the similarities between these two asteroids exceed the differences. Both asteroids can be involved in any kind of Libra activity, any variety of ongoing cooperative or competitive relationships. Both Juno and Pallas seem to represent the fighting side of Libra and the seventh house, which Venus has never fully explained. Juno and Pallas appear to demand the justice and full equality of Libra, so they are often clues to relationships where there is tension.

It is possible that their entrance into astrology at the moment when gender equality began to gain ground is an indication that they are keys to that movement. The entrance of Ceres and Vesta into astrological usage may signify the need to return to the old work ethic of Virgo—doing a good job for its own sake, rather than for some extrinsic reward. All the asteroids may be indicative of craftsmanship and artistic skills that are found with both Virgo and Libra.

Much work must be done before we can validate these descriptions of the four asteroids, but they have proved highly valuable in the time they have been available, and seem well worth adding to the astrologer's tool kit. Eventually, we will have many more to investigate. The four now available are only the first to be discovered among thousands of these little planets.

Vertex Axis

Another relatively little used factor in astrology is the third angle-axis, the Vertex-AntiVertex. The usual angles include the Ascendant-Descendant axis which is formed by the intersection of the ecliptic with the rational horizon, and the Midheaven-fourth house cusp axis (MC-IC), which is derived from the intersection of the ecliptic with the birth Meridian. The third angle-axis, the Vertex-AntiVertex, comes from the intersection of the ecliptic with the Prime Vertical.

This axis may fall anywhere across the chart with the Vertex always the western end. Most of the time, the Vertex is in the fifth to the eighth houses. To calculate the Vertex, subtract the latitude of birth from 90 degrees to get the co-latitude of birth. The IC of the chart (fourth house cusp) is then used as an MC, and for that MC, the Ascendant at the co-latitude is the Vertex. The Anti-Vertex is always exactly opposite the Vertex. The symbol for the Vertex is "Vx."

The meaning of the Vertex axis seems to be somewhat similar to the Ascendant-Descendant and also somewhat like the Nodes of the Moon.

We tend to be involved with relationships with these polar oppositions. The Anti-Vertex, like the Ascendant, points to the individual's own desires and actions, while the Vertex symbolizes others in the life of the person, and to some extent, conditions outside of personal control.

Everything in the chart actually provides information on the individual, but most people are attracted to others who manifest those qualities shown by the seventh and eighth houses. The Vertex appears to be another key to the qualities that we may project into others.

The Vertex axis is like the Nodes of the Moon in that both are polar oppositions where the individual must seek to integrate the polarity. The Nodes can be considered a primary key to a lesson area, with the South Node the more challenging as a general rule. Where the South Node falls, we have something to learn, and once learned, something to give. Somewhat similarly, the Vertex may represent a lesson area where we learn through our relationships with others.

Dwads and Decanates

There are many other potentially valuable factors used by astrology, but the tools described here seem to be the most basic. Other forms of the astrological alphabet include the subdivisions of zodiacal signs into decanates of 10 degrees each and into dwads of 2½ degrees each.

The modern interpretation of decanates suggests that the first third of each sign represents the pure nature of the sign, that the second third carries overtones of the next sign of the same element, and that the last third of the sign carries the qualities of the last sign of the element. For example, the first third of Aries would be pure Aries; the middle third would have Leo tendencies; and the last third would have Sagittarius overtones.

Dwads apply the same principle to divisions of the signs into 12 sections of 2½ degrees each. The whole zodiac is represented in each sign with the subtle additional shading associated with the following signs in the natural order of the zodiac. For example, the first 2½ degrees of Aries are considered pure Aries, Aries carries some Taurus tendencies from 2½ to 5 degrees of Aries carries some Taurus tendencies, 5 to 7½ degrees is colored a little by Gemini, 7½ to 10 degrees has Cancer overtones, and so on. Each time a new decanate starts, the dwad of the 2½ degrees is associated with the same sign. Ten to 12½ degrees of Aries is both the Leo dwad and part of the Leo decanate.

Planetary Nodes

The nodes of the planets also seem to be a variant of the basic alphabet of astrology. Mars' nodes carry the qualities of Mars; Venus' nodes those of Venus; and so on. My book, *The Node Book*, covers these in more detail, including the Moon's Nodes in the six polarities of the zodiac. The South Node seems usually more stressful, indicating areas of lessons or challenges. Exact aspects to the Nodes can be read as similar to a weak version of the same aspect to the planet whose Node is involved.

The Node Book also provides the geocentric positions of the planetary nodes. Most books give the heliocentric positions, which are relatively stationary. Geocentric, of course, means as seen from the position of Earth, while heliocentric means as seen from the sun.

As the Earth moves in its orbit, it will see the planetary nodes in different parts of the zodiac, if we define the nodes as the intersections of another planet's orbit with the plane of Earth's orbit. This is especially true for the nodes of the inner planets, Venus and Mercury. At times these will line up with the sun so that both south and north nodes are conjunct each other and the Sun. This marks an area of enormous emphasis in the life.

However, if we think of the nodes as the intersection two orbital planes, with the resulting "line of nodes," projected to infinity, the Earth and sun's viewpoints merge and the heliocentric nodes can be included in a geocentric chart.

Fixed Stars

The fixed stars may provide still another form of the astrological alphabet if the ancient traditions are accurate in assigning the qualities of one or two planets to each of the major stars. Insufficient work has been done to be sure of this assignment, but it is an area worth testing. Work to date suggests that some of the traditional associations with the stars do have validity, but that they need not be as negative as usually portrayed. The events connected with the stars are no longer as prevalent as when these associations were originally made.

Modern experience seems to point to a conjunction with a bright star as a key to prominence of some sort, but whether the emphasis will be pleasant or painful depends on the individual's level of consciousness. There are positive alternatives to all of the factors in astrology.

Midpoints and Arabic Parts

Midpoints and Arabic Parts, both derived by combining other factors in the chart, offer still another tool of considerable value. The reality of these additional sensitive points in the chart is amply documented.

In general, it is possible to read these extra points as a combination of the factors from which they are derived. Thus, the midpoint of Sun and Moon, usually written as Sun/Moon, is similar to a weak version of a conjunction of the Sun and Moon. Midpoints are like a latent potential that can be activated by an aspect from a planet, asteroid, angle, etc.

Arabic Parts, which result from adding two factors and subtracting a third, seem to represent a point where there is a combination of the added factors without the presence of the one subtracted.

For example, the Part of Fortune, which is much used in astrology, is calculated by adding the Moon to the Ascendant and subtracting the Sun. The name is a poor translation of the Latin word *Fortuna*, which means Fate.

The sign and house of the Part of Fortune are neither lucky nor unlucky in their own nature, but they seem to represent automatic habit patterns or talents or tendencies present from the beginning of the life before the expansive ego drive of the Sun has begun to operate. Growth to the full potential of the Sun may diminish the emphasis on the activity associated with the Part of Fortune, but if there are aspects between the Sun and Fortuna, the activity may be continued and increased as life goes on.

Of course this makes one wonder about Arabic Parts such as the Part of Marriage, which adds the Ascendant and Descendant (appropriate for getting together with a potential partner) but takes away Venus. Marriage without love or happiness?

Sorting the Alphabet Soup

In all the preceding pages, we have continued to accumulate the very details discussed in the beginning as a threat to our goal of finding a living human being. Brief attempts at synthesis and the integration of all these details have been discussed in the sections on elements and qualities, and the dilemmas. In the latter section, we mentioned the variety of ways in which the freedom-closeness dilemma could be shown. There are numerous other ways in which the different astrological letters may be combined or contrasted, to show emphasis on a part of life.

The twelve parts of life can be thought of as three sections of four letters each (planets, signs, and houses). The first four letters represent personal needs. There is often a childlike, spontaneous quality where these are emphasized in people. Life is met as if it were new, fresh, uncomplicated. The middle third of the zodiac represents the need for and/or the capacity for interpersonal relationships. Where these planets, signs, or houses are emphasized, marriage and family may take precedence over the rest of life. Actually, to be most accurate, Moon, Cancer, and the fourth house should be included with the interpersonal letters. Cancer is initially the baby looking for a mother, but with maturity becomes the mother looking for a baby. Dependency becomes nurturance as the individual shifts from the family of orientation to the family of procreation.

Virgo, in contrast, lacks the personal feelings associated with the other interpersonal letters. Getting the job done efficiently is the primary goal. Virgo represents interpersonal relationships connected to work, coworkers, and those who work for us. The final third of the zodiac indicates the impersonal parts of life. Here we deal with society as a whole, and with humanity in a partially abstract way—with abstract learning that goes beyond the here-and-now focus of Gemini. Where the planets or signs of the personal letters are placed in the houses of the impersonal, or vice versa, the individual may seek to satisfy interpersonal needs through service to humanity.

The contrast between freedom (a life with minimal close ties and obligations from personal relationships) and the need for close relationships can be seen by mixed emphasis on one or more of the "free" letters (Aries, Sagittarius, Aquarius), plus emphasis on the signs requiring personal involvement (Cancer, Leo, Libra, Scorpio). Signs alone are listed for convenience, but planets and houses should be assumed as carrying the same meaning, referring to the same basic human drives.

Although all the earth letters represent the drive to affect the physical world, letters 6 and 10 are especially the workers, symbolizing all the Puritan virtues. But Virgo and Capricorn may also be combined with Scorpio and thought of as the three obsessive-compulsive letters. All three have an inordinate need for order and organization, a tendency to have a mind like a filing cabinet, with masses of useful data stored away. When these three letters are overdone, there may be an extreme need to have a place for everything and everything in its place.

Serious anxiety, depression, phobias, etc. are most likely to be present with combinations of letters 4, 10, and 12. Cancer and Pisces, unless strengthened by other factors, tend to look to others for security, and thus fall prey to insecurity and inadequacy feelings. Capricorn, as key to the power of the world to put limits on us, is often a clue to inner anxiety. A strong person will work to the top to find reassurance by having the power partially under personal control.

If the chart is too overloaded with the dependent water factors plus a heavy dose of letter 10, especially including a negatively aspected Saturn or tenth house, or planets in Capricorn, the individual is likely to be subject to serious anxiety, depression, repression, etc. The best antidote is fire, which symbolizes faith in oneself or in life. Air factors are also helpful since they permit the individual to be detached and objective and rational about the situation, hopefully finding an intelligent solution.

Still another combination can come with letters 2, 7, and 12. These are the keys to love of beauty and capacity to create it in life. Venus and its signs and houses represent love and pleasure and beauty at the human level, while Neptune and its sign and house symbolize the search for infinite love and beauty. Combinations of these factors may show really creative artists. The danger of such mixtures, as already indicated, can be a tendency to idealize love and to expect more of human relationships than is possible to attain. But where the individual simply values love and beauty enough to work for them, the combinations are highly fulfilling.

A high level of mechanical ability can be shown by combinations of Mars, Mercury, and Uranus, including their signs and houses, of course. There may be much interest in modern technological developments and skill in coordination and the use of tools. Mars-Mercury mixtures often produce the "tongue like a sword." Jupiter-Mercury mixtures frequently show an individual who believes in "the truth at any cost." They tend to have a sharp sense of humor, but sometimes a glaring lack of tact. Mars-Jupiter marks the athlete or sportsman and occasionally the gambler.

There are many keys to intelligence, including all the air letters in addition to Virgo and Sagittarius. All the water letters show potential involvement with the subconscious, which may include good memory, psychic ability, and capacity for spiritual healing. Fire letters have been mentioned as being especially creative, but this is due in part to their tendency to have faith in themselves so that they are willing to try something new and to act from their own center, from their own individuality.

Is Once Enough?

One of the basic facts of astrology is that anything that is important in the character will be said repeatedly in the chart. You will find charts that repeat the same theme as many as eight or more times. Astrology is probably the most complex and sophisticated method of describing life that has ever been discovered or developed by human beings. The whole pattern never repeats, and yet this infinite variability is achieved with the different forms of the twelve-letter alphabet, interweaving twelve sides of life. Astrology offers a never-ending challenge and fascination—a mirror of life to those with eyes to see and minds to comprehend.

Chapter Seven

The Alphabet in Action

> *"Having come this far in our examination of astrological theories, can we actually take a horoscope and find the person hidden there?"*

Having come this far in our examination of astrological theories, can we actually take a horoscope and find the person hidden there? Tennis star Billie Jean's King autobiography includes her full birth data.

Looking at Billie's horoscope, what can we deduce? What are the major themes in the chart? A drive for power and prominence comes through loud and clear. Capricorn is rising, with Mars conjunct Saturn in the Sun house, while the Sun is in the Saturn house. This is a combination of letters 1, 5, and 10—personal self-will in action, need to pour out energy to have an impact on the world and to get an emotional response in return, and need to be in control of the life.

Adding still further emphasis to this theme are the planet Uranus and the asteroid Vesta in the Sun (Leo) house and four factors in

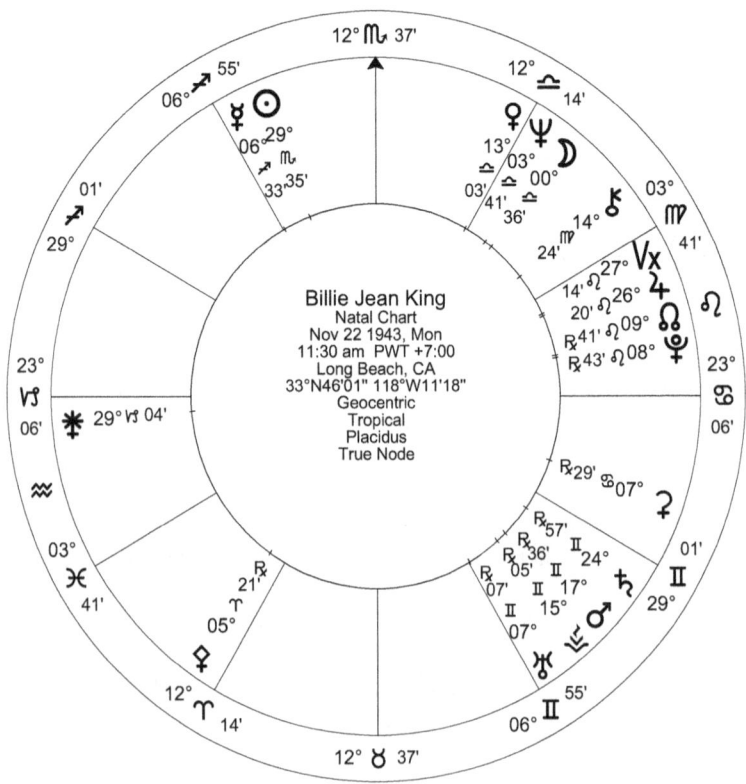

Billie Jean King

the sign of Leo (Pluto, North Node, Jupiter, and the Vertex) all in the seventh (Libra) house. The importance of Leo is also shown by the elevated Sun and the active fifth house. This Leo power indicates a natural leader, actress, and promoter, with a strong potential for showmanship and magnetism.

Still other factors repeat the theme of power over others or suggest an attraction toward competitive interactions. Libra-Aries mixtures, as well as emphasis on Libra and Scorpio, show such an attraction. Note that both of the asteroids tentatively assigned to Libra are connected to Aries-Juno in the Aries house and Pallas in the Aries sign. In addition to the four factors already listed in the house of Libra, the Moon, Neptune, and Venus are in the sign of Libra in the house of Scorpio. The Sun is in the sign of Scorpio.

Letters 7 and 8 (Libra-Scorpio) represent our capacity to relate to peers in persisting contacts. The relationship may be cooperative or competitive. The greater the emphasis on these parts of life, whether shown by the rulers being prominent or by the signs and houses being occupied, the more strongly the person is apt to center the life in related actions.

Too much focus on letters 7 and 8 often indicates an insecure or defensive person. In a strong individual, however, they show a competitive nature, which may be successfully directed into business, sports, military service, and similar professions. Acting, politics, and law are also possibilities, with the entertainment field especially likely if Leo is featured in the chart.

The general air-fire emphasis shown by grand trines in both elements indicates a person whose life is much involved with others. There is a keen sense of humor and love of fun, a quick-witted mind and the quick tongue of a salesperson—the restlessness, versatility, and verbal fluency of this hot air combination. Plus enough openness to share her birth data, for which we give thanks. Friends and new knowledge are likely to be highly valued with Mercury in Sagittarius in the eleventh house. Venus in the ninth house in Libra shows pleasure from travel, especially when shared.

The strength of the air in the chart probably helps to temper the power drive—the need to be one-up. Libra values justice and fair play. Aquarius seeks equality. So long as there is a healthy outlet such as sports, games, or business for the competitive side of the nature, there is less danger of this competitive spirit creeping into relationships, which should be cooperative.

Even with this outlet, however, it will be necessary to work at the cooperative associations such as marriage and business if they are to be sustained. The axes of the Nodes and Vertex across the first and seventh houses show the tendency to pull apart in personal relationships. To have harmony with others, the personal will must be modified to meet the desires of others.

These oppositions across letters 1-7 and 5-11 are present with both signs and houses, and represent variations on the freedom-closeness dilemma. Cancer, Leo, Libra, and Scorpio are all occupied by sign, and all except Cancer by house, showing the strong desire for personal relationships. At the same time, all the "free-soul" signs and houses are occupied—Aries, Sagittarius, and Aquarius. A compromise is obviously necessary for full satisfaction in life.

With Ceres in Cancer in the sixth house, some of the nurturance potential of the nature may be satisfied in contacts with fellow workers. Normally, a full fifth house indicates an urge toward motherhood, but with Saturn, Mars, and Vesta there, the career may take precedence over progeny. Saturn is the natural ruler of the tenth house of career. Mars rules the tenth house in this chart. Vesta is a key to work as the ruler of Virgo and is especially prone to pull back from personal relationships in order to give the whole life to a career.

Another way to analyze a chart involves a consideration of early role models such as parents and siblings. The interchange in this chart of Sun (ruling Leo, which is present in the seventh house) placed in the tenth house and Pluto (ruler of the MC) placed in the seventh house, shows a parent as role model for partnership.

Venus ruling the IC and placed in Libra; Moon, natural ruler of the fourth house, also in Libra; and Cancer, natural sign of the fourth house on the cusp of the seventh house, all repeat the theme of a 4-7-10 mixture. Such combinations warn against turning a peer relationship into a parent-child association. It is important that each partner be able to give and receive so there is interdependency.

Although there are relatively few squares in this chart, the Sun's square to Jupiter and the Vertex axis occurs in fixed signs in cardinal houses, reminding us of the danger of life as a perpetual power struggle. Sometimes it is helpful to analyze the early relationships with parents when authority figures appear to be involved in peer adjustments.

Capricorn rising (as well as Mars conjunct Saturn) normally indicates a personal identification with the father or a father substitute. This identification may be positive or negative, depending on whether father represents what the subject wants to become or hopes to avoid. Father is also role model in the search for love and ego needs since Saturn is in the fifth house.

A sibling may also have been a role model, both for self and for love needs, with Mars ruling the third house and in the fifth. Mars in or ruling the third or fourth houses is often a key to sibling rivalry, sometimes for parental affection. Just putting Mars and Saturn together shows the tendency toward either overdrive or self-blocking. In this chart, it would most certainly be overdrive, and analysis of early experiences might help to clarify the motivational dynamics.

Remember, we have major themes centered around both power and freedom, and these do tend to support each other to some degree since freedom can be described as the avoidance of being dominated. Capricorn in the first house and Mars conjunct Saturn (two forms of the same principle) may indicate a desire to be in control of oneself or to avoid being controlled.

An insecure person may be striving to gain a sense of self-worth while a strong individual is making personal will into law. If the child is identified with the father-figure, as is normal, she may want to be like him, to be his opposite, to win his approval by reaching the heights, to surpass him and put him down, or any other related drives.

To sum up, this is certainly a chart with an outgoing and active life involving many people. This is a warm person; a driving person with a capacity for sustained energy as is indicated by a bit of the steamroller Sun in the Saturn house; Saturn in the Sun house; Mars conjunction Saturn; Capricorn in the Aries house.

There is likely to be considerable monetary success, although the individual may spend it almost as fast as it comes in, with fire in the second house. But there will probably always be more. Fire knows what it wants and has the power to go get it, especially when backed by a bit of practical earth and quick witted and versatile air. All in all, the chart looks like a successful person and a fun person. Just don't get in the way of the steamroller.

Chapter Eight

Ethical Astrology

"As a final word, I would like to emphasize that the first goal of humanistic astrology is to find the person behind the mass of details in the chart. The second goal is to help that person."

So much more might be said. The complexities of astrology are endless. But the basics have been presented here, and the art of synthesis can only be learned by working with charts. There is no substitute for practice. As a final word, I would like to emphasize that the first goal of humanistic astrology is to find the person behind the mass of details in the chart. The second goal is to help that person. To do this, it is important to always offer hope.

There is no factor or combination of factors without a positive potential. It is the astrologer's task to find the positive alternatives to the problem manifestations. For a fully effective job, mutual confidence is needed—a sharing between astrologer and client. The horoscope shows the general outline of the personality dynamics, but the details of manifestation can vary depending on the degree to which the subject has self-awareness and self-mastery. It is the little daily choices that eventually determine character and destiny. It is only necessary to change the angle of the wheel of a car one inch for it to end up in a totally different place.

Remember that the information you give to another person becomes part of your own karma. The astrologer's task is to facilitate understanding of life and the cosmos so that clients can make wiser decisions. It is not the task of the counselor to decide for clients and to try to push them into action. Unless you have a sincere desire to help others, and a basic faith in life, astrology may not be the best field for you. Astrology can either build people up or tear them down. We all need to have faith in ourselves and you will sleep better at night if the people who come to you leave with greater faith.

Appendix I
The Astrological Alphabet

House-Planet-Sign Combinations

House	Planet		Sign		Element	Quality
1 (+)	♂	Mars	♈	Aries	Fire	Cardinal
2 (−)	♀	Venus	♉	Taurus	Earth	Fixed
3 (+)	☿	Mercury	♊	Gemini	Air	Mutable
4 (−)	☽	Moon	♋	Cancer	Water	Cardinal
5 (+)	☉	Sun	♌	Leo	Fire	Fixed
6 (−)	☿	Mercury	♍	Virgo	Earth	Mutable
7 (+)	♀	Venus	♎	Libra	Air	Cardinal
8 (−)	♇	Pluto	♏	Scorpio	Water	Fixed
9 (+)	♃	Jupiter	♐	Sagittarius	Fire	Mutable
10 (−)	♄	Saturn	♑	Capricorn	Earth	Cardinal
11 (+)	♅	Uranus	♒	Aquarius	Air	Fixed
12 (−)	♆	Neptune	♓	Pisces	Water	Mutable

Each line shares the same key meaning, e.g. the first house, Mars, and Aries are cardinal fire and symbolize direct self-expression, self-will in action.

The use of the terms "positive" and "negative" in astrology is similar to their use in electricity, with no connotation of "good" and "bad." Positive signs (air and fire) are said to be active, open, spontaneous, oriented to outward expression. Negative signs (earth and water) are reactive, concealing, deliberate, serious, oriented to preservation and retention.Although the three outer and more recently discovered planets have been assigned to rulership of three signs, the traditional rulers of these signs must still be taken into account in reading houses of the chart ruled by them. These are Jupiter as co-ruler of Pisces, Saturn as co-ruler of Aquarius, and Mars as co-ruler of Scorpio. Also, four asteroids, discovered between Mars and Jupiter, are proving valuable. Ceres and Vesta seem to share the rulership of Virgo with Mercury, while Pallas and Juno share the rulership of Libra with Venus.

Key Phrases for House-Planet-Sign Combinations

First-Aries-Mars
"I do my thing."

Free self-expression; self-will in spontaneous action; initiative, impulse, courage, pioneering spirit, vitality, skilled coordination, enthusiasm for the new, ready to fight against any limits on personal freedom.

Second-Taurus-Venus
"I enjoy the sense world."

Pleasure in manipulating the physical sense world; comfort, security, contentment, love of beauty in tangible possessions; deliberate, persisting determination, slow to become angry and to forget.

Third-Gemini-Mercury
"I see, conceptualize and talk."

Consciousness, capacity to learn and communicate; thought, language, contact with nearby equals, dexterity, curiosity, versatility, multiple interests, flexibility, cheerful, witty, flippant.

Fourth-Cancer-Moon
"I save, protect, nourish and assimilate."

The personal unconscious; memory; dependence or nurturance; absorption, protection, preservation, sensitivity, empathy, need for warmth and emotional closeness and rootedness.

Fifth-Leo-Sun
"I rejoice in projecting my personal power into the world."

Ego-expansion and creativity; urge to transcend the past, to be in the limelight, to win admiration, applause, love; enthusiasm, joy, drama, leader ship, magnetism, generosity, pride.

Sixth-Virgo-Mercury
"I work competently."

Efficient functioning in one's job and in one's body; focus on flaws in order to correct them; service; productive work; analysis, discrimination, pragmatism, quiet efficiency, attention to detail; self-restraint, humility, interest in health and healing.

Seventh-Libra-Venus
"I enjoy balance."

Partnership, cooperation or competition with equals; justice, both sides in balance; harmony, arbitration, pleasure from grace, line, form, a feeling for space, and for interaction with peers; need for "equal to others" to feel complete.

Eighth-Scorpio-Pluto
"I share the sense world with others for mutual pleasure and seek self-knowledge and self-mastery."

Self-knowledge learned through the mirror of a mate and self-mastery learned out of respect for the rights of the mate; ability to give, to receive, and to share for mutual satisfaction; passionate intensity; learning what is ours and what belongs to someone else, how to love and yet let go, when to stop, to discard the outgrown past.

Ninth-Sagittarius-Jupiter
"I trust, value and direct my life according to my understanding."

Search for the intellectual absolute, philosophical, religious and ethical belief systems; definition of what is real, true, morally right, and valuable, the basis for choices and goals; trust, optimism, humor, generosity, expansiveness; love of books, or travel, or nature, or sports, depending on the definition of value; the urge to reach further.

Tenth-Capricorn-Saturn
"I carry out the law."

Law—karmic, natural, manmade—what we can do, what we can't do, what we must do; the nature of the world which sets the outer limits to self-will, and the conscience which sets inner limits; the Puritan virtues—duty, responsibility, thrift, practicality, realism; the need for power and achievement, either to feel secure from the world's threat, to attain a sense of self-worth, or to avoid guilt; crystallized structure from social institutions to bones and teeth.

Eleventh-Aquarius-Uranus
"I seek to expand knowledge and freedom for all humanity."

Voluntary community without coercion; everyone equalitarian, open, individualistic, accepting; the search for new knowledge; rebellion against tradition or any other limitation in order to facilitate growth; explosive struggle against routine or restriction.

Twelfth-Pisces-Neptune
"I dream of love and beauty and am absorbed in the whole."

Search for emotional absolutes, for infinite love and beauty; the mystic who is one with the whole; sensitivity, empathy, compassion, creative imagination, fantasy, the artist, the savior, or the victim seeking an easy road to the great vision through drugs, alcohol, psychosis, or invalidism; moving toward the vision or waiting for the world to give it.

Major Aspects

☌ *Conjunction*
Degrees Apart: 0
Fraction of Circle: 0
Nature: Depends on planets, sign, and house involved, and other aspects to the conjunction.
Orb (tentative): 10-12
Power: Very strong

⚺ *Semisextile*
Degrees Apart: 30
Fraction of Circle: 1/12
Nature: Potential harmony
Orb (tentative): 3
Power: Weak

∠ *Semisquare*
Degrees Apart: 45
Fraction of Circle: 1/8
Nature: Friction
Orb (tentative): 5
Power: Moderate

✶ *Sextile*
Degrees Apart: 60
Fraction of Circle: 1/6
Nature: Harmony, opportunity
Orb (tentative): 7
Power: Moderate

□ *Square*
Degrees Apart: 90
Fraction of Circle: 1/4
Nature: Stress, conflict
Orb (tentative): 8-10
Power: Strong

△ *Trine*
Degrees Apart: 120
Fraction of Circle: 1/3
Nature: Harmony, talent
Orb (tentative): 8-10
Power: Strong

⚼ *Sesquisquare*
Degrees Apart: 135
Fraction of Circle: 3/8
Nature: Friction
Orb (tentative): 5
Power: Moderate

⚻ *Inconjunct or Quincunx*
Degrees Apart: 150
Fraction of Circle: 5/12
Nature: Strain, separation, adjustment
Orb (tentative): 3
Power: Strong

☍ *Opposition*
Degrees Apart: 180
Fraction of Circle: 1/2
Nature: Separation or cooperation
Orb (tentative): 8-10
Power: Strong

∥ *Parallel*
Degrees Apart: 0
Fraction of Circle: Same declination
Nature: Similar to weak conjunction
Orb (tentative): 1
Power: Moderate

⚃ *Anti-parallel*
Degrees Apart: 0
Fraction of Circle: Opposite declination
Nature: Similar to weak opposition
Orb (tentative): 1
Power: Moderate

Minor Aspects

All of the below aspects were developed by Kepler and are based on division of the circle by fifths. All are said to be mildly harmonious, with creative potential. Orb is limited to 2 degrees or less, and they are very weak unless exact.

Vigintile
Degrees Apart: 18
Fraction of Circle: 1/20

Decile
Degrees Apart: 36
Fraction of Circle: 1/10

Quintile
Degrees Apart: 72
Fraction of Circle: 1/5

Tredecile
Degrees Apart: 108
Fraction of Circle: 3/10

Biquintile
Degrees Apart: 144
Fraction of Circle: 2/5

The following minor aspects are very weak. They have a 1-degree orb and are not in common use.

Undecagon
Degrees Apart: 33+
Fraction of Circle: 1/11

Nonagon
Degrees Apart: 40
Fraction of Circle: 1/9

Septile
Degrees Apart: 51+
Fraction of Circle: 1/7

Harmonics

These aspects are 7½, 11¼, and 18 degrees apart. John Nelson's forecasts of ionospheric disturbances support aspects for every multiple of 7½, 11¼, and 18 degrees. These aspects should be limited to a 1-degree orb and are probably only significant when involved in combinations with traditional aspects.

The general question of orb of influence for all aspects may have to be left undecided until further research is available.

Zip Dobyns receives the Lifetime Achievement Award from ISAR (International Society for Astrological Research).

Zipporah Pottenger Dobyns received her Ph.D. in clinical psychology and was also certified as a professional astrologer (1960) by the American Federation of Astrologers (and by International Society of Astrological Research when they developed a certification program). Zip was also a minister in the Community Church of Religious Science. She lectured and gave workshops all over the world and held many Astrological Intensives that lasted from 10 to 16 days—teaching astrology and psychology to students in Canada, Mexico, the United States, Australia, and New Zealand.

Zip won numerous astrological awards from her peers, including Best Lecturer (Virgo) at AFA many times, two Regulus Awards from ISAR (for Research and Innovation and for Teaching), the coveted Southern Cross from the Federation of Australian Astrologers, Outstanding Contribution to the Art & Science of Astrology from Professional Astrologers Incorporated, Service to Astrology from Aquarius Workshops, and the Lifetime Achievement Award from International Society from Astrological Research.

A prolific writer, Zip authored a number of books including (1977) *The Asteroid Ephemeris*; (1973) *Astrologer's Casebook* (with Nancy Roof); (1996) *The Book of Saturn*; (1972) *Distance Values*; (1972) *Evolution through the Zodiac*; (1983) *Expanding Astrology's Universe*; (1973) *Finding the Person in the Horoscope*; (2002) *Healing Mother/Daughter Relationships* (with Maritha Pottenger); (1973) *The Node Book*; (1994) *Planets on the Move* (with Maritha Pottenger); (1975) *Progressions, Directions and Rectification*; (1985) *Seven Paths to Understanding* (with William Wrobel); (1998) *Unveiling your Future* (with Maritha Pottenger); and (1977) *The Zodiac as a Key to History*. Her book of poetry (*God's World*) was published in 1957 and she was working on children's poems (unpublished) before her passing in the summer of 2003.

Zip contributed to numerous astrological (and some psychological) journals, including *The Mutable Dilemma* and *Asteroid World* (now available online through ccrsdodona.org) for which she wrote the majority of the articles for 25 years.

Zip had four children of her flesh, three of whom were active in the astrological world (and the fourth in healing). Many of her students considered Zip to be their spiritual mother, and asked to be in the family next lifetime. (She had a first-house Moon, strong Ceres and Mars in the fourth house, so was very nurturing and a mother figure to many.) She is deeply missed.

www.ingramcontent.com/pod-product-compliance
Lightning Source LLC
Chambersburg PA
CBHW051714040426
42446CB00008B/883